DEGAS

BY EDUARD HÜTTINGER

CROWN PUBLISHERS, INC. · NEW YORK

1960

Title page: SELF PORTRAIT OF DEGAS (Detail). Oil, 1855 $(31^{7}/_{6}"\times25^{1}/_{4}")$
Musée du Louvre, Paris

Translated by:

ELLEN HEALY

PRINTED IN ITALY

YOUNG SPARTANS EXERCISING (43½" × 62") 1860. National Gallery, London.

To M. M.

Edgar Degas takes a place in 19th Century French Painting which is not at all easy to define precisely and briefly. Most of the great painters of the 19th Century can be identified with one of the particular trends of period, so that the essential features of these masters are clearly revealed. Ingres is identified with Classicism; Delacroix with Romanticism; Courbet with Realism; Monet, Sisley, Pissarro and, less distinctively, yet in certain important aspects, Manet and Renoir with Impressionism; Seurat and Signac within Neo-impressionism. Degas, however, stands in a category by himself. Although he follows in part the classical style of Ingres, shows touches of Realism, and to a greater extent of Impressionism, he never identifies himself completely with any one of these trends. He maintains his independence in human, artistic, and technical respects. He obeys the laws of his own development in the solitude of his studio; he feels compelled to follow an individual law of growth to a greater extent than anyone else, except Cézanne, although the two differed greatly in detail. Degas and Cézanne are — each, however, in a radically different way — great, independent personalities in 19th Century painting, an epoch, that is marked by the formation of groups of similar artists. Considered in the light of sequence of style, which rules 19th Century French Painting — and the beginning of the 20th

5

Century, Degas' art covers a field which extends from Classicism to Fauvism. Through none of the styles characteristic of the 19th Century can a lead be found to the understanding of this art; its conditions, its source lie in the core of the personality of the man and artist, Degas. Lastly, as a result of the upheaval caused by the French Revolution, the original functional unity of art and religion was finally destroyed for reasons which will not be discussed here. With the Revolution, art broke away from the mythical concept. Europe's social structure which, until that time had represented a rigid system, was dissolved. The artist's destiny became increasingly one of isolation and segregation.

It is true that, on the surface, Ingres was able to acquire a social position as Director of the Academy in Rome, and was later able to maintain his position as the bearer of certain honourable titles, traditionally due to an important artist; artistically, too, he established a link with a great heritage in Classicism. Delacroix, meanwhile, was able to commune with the most significant works in the literature and art of the past, in his own personal way, at the expense of cutting himself off from the masses and creating works whose Christian and mythological themes were no longer in tune with the times — and these prove their vitality alone through a form of art that is completely selfcontained and moved by pathos and melancholy. In the world outside the spiritual trend in history had already reached a climax before 1850 yet by the middle of the 19th Century, all important artistic work was done in complete and utter isolation and loneliness. Ingres' Classicism which had also become a school in its own right, underwent a change in the form of the barren and academic Ecole des Beaux-Arts. Romantic Painting, however, was not destined to create a school of lasting influence.

This is the situation in which Degas found himself. For a short time he adhered to the « Classical School »; later however, he broke away from the traditional pattern and created quite a personal iconography of his own, which revolved round three centres: the world of the theatre, the ballet and the racecourse, while landscapes, seen through a clear unproblematic eye, predominate in the art of the programmatic Impressionists. Degas never considered himself a painter of lanscapes. Nature — and by this term we mean everything nature can offer as a subject for painting — meant nothing to him; and he cared just as little for artistically-arranged and cultivated nature which still life offered. With an extraordinary intensity he registered the strangest and most unusual position of the human body through the medium of a precise, though extremely vivid sketch. Last, but not least, he differs from his contemporaries by giving to drawing the primary place in all artistic creation. This power in his drawing is, in the last analysis, based on Degas' respect for the old masters. In a classic form of expression, the highly developed line, Degas catches contemporary « modern life » in its spontaneous expression, and, in so doing, immortalizes it. These paradoxes that his works contain are clearly expressed by the words written by the young Degas himself in one of his notebooks: « O Giotto, do not stand before the picture of Paris, and Paris do not obscure Giotto's picture ». Thus, Degas has named the two components which are present in his art, and which constantly permeate each other: the great western tradition of Classicism, plus his passionately direct interpretation of the essential phenomena of his own present existence.

The loneliness which besets Degas' entire life and which is an integral part of his existence, as is the case only with Cézanne, is based not only on the spiritual structure of the epoch but, also arises out of Degas' own personality. In his letters, which repeatedly stress the fact that he has to be alone with his work, he perhaps, at first, makes a virtue of his distress at not being understood, the indifference which surrounds him and the resistence he had to face in those circles which formerly supported art.

6

Portrait of Marguerite Degas. Pencil. Musée du Louvre, Paris.

In the last analysis, these letters exactly reflect the factual reality in which, and out of which, Degas has created his work. The loneliness which came of self-realization explains almost all the aspects of his character which were perceived and handed down by his contemporaries. His sarcasm « which drove him to witty aperçus » (1) and so often offended, and his character, both thoroughly irritable and sceptical, were the reason why people accused him of insensitivity and coldness, and why his friendship with artist colleagues was often endangered. However, the picture Vollard draws of Degas is, without doubt, badly done and borders on a caricature. The extremely conscientious and painstaking George Rivière comes much closer to the truth when he speaks of a « false misanthrop »; everything — this cutting coldness, this cruelty and acute perception which could lay men bare — everything was really only the veneer of self-protection beneath which lay an easily-wounded heart. As an artist, Degas enjoyed indisputably high esteem among his close colleagues and friends, in spite of personal quarrels from time to time. This applies to Manet as well as to Renoir, Monet and Guillemet, Gauguin and Van Gogh. Finally, Degas strongly influenced the art of his time without ever wishing to — suffice it to mention names like Manet, Mary Cassatt, Forain, Gauguin, Lautrec, Suzanne Valadon, Vuillard. He was faithful to the end to the comrades of his youth, Paul Valpinçon, Henri and Alexis Rouart.

His point of view concerning the Dreyfuss affair was the result of his aristocratic, conservative attitude, his loathing of mass-movements and modern democracy. It also sprang from his anti-semitism. Although it brought about his separation from Ludovic Halévy and from Monet, the sculptor Bartholomé remained one of his closest friends till the end. He was consistent in his opinion that people should not know about his love-affairs — let alone his escapades. Degas' life in the sphere of human relations therefore appears marked by a certain uneventfulness. This uneventfulness, however, this, as it were, unfulfilled fate, was the prerequisite for the freedom of his art, the price he had to pay. He stated the following principle and abided by it throughout his life: « One must have a high opinion of a work of art — not of the art one is creating at the moment, but of that which one desires to achieve one day. Without this it is not worthwhile working » (2).

Edgar-Hilaire-Germain de Gas was born in Paris in rue Saint Georges, on July 19th, 1834, the child of a wealthy upper-middle-class Parisian, but the grandchild of an Italian grandmother. His grandfather, Hilaire-René de Gas, had fled from France during the Revolution; in Naples he discovered a new home, founding a bank and marrying a local girl. Degas' father, Auguste, came to Paris when he was young, to set up a branch of the business and it was here that he made the acquaintance of Célestine Musson, (3) who came of a Creole family of French descent and who became his wife. It is surprising that Edgar Degas should not be of pure French lineage, living as he did in Paris, and by the inspiration it gave him. His concept of art contains the essence of the Parisian to an extent achieved by no other painter except Manet. In all probability, it was his foreign blood — the de Gas family were related to the Italian aristocracy, among them Baroness Bellelli and Duchess Morbilli — which enabled him to see the fundamental aspects of Parisian life and to depict it with detachment in precise perspective.

Degas spent his youth in wealthy and cultured surroundings; his father, the banker was interested in the arts and, above all, a music-lover. As the eldest son, Edgar was to have taken over the banking

1) WILHELM HAUSSENSTEIN, *Degas,* Bern 1948, p. 12.
2) FRANCOIS FOSCA, *Degas,* Geneva 1954, p. 97.
3) Up until 1873 he signed his name, on his pictures as well, with the aristocratic spelling « de Gas. Later he simplified it to « Degas ».

Portrait of Mademoiselle Fiocre in the Ballet « La Source. » Oil, 1868. (52" × 67½")
Brooklyn Museum, New York

THE DAUGHTER OF JEPTHAH. Oil, 1864. Smith College Museum, Northampton, Mass.

business and his studies were therefore intended to equip him for a lawyer's career. However, he proved to be a bad pupil; only in drawing did he have good marks. As a school-boy he was obsessed by his dream of becoming an artist, and finally, after tenaciously insisting on his plan, he was allowed by his father to realize his dream.

His transition to an artist's life did not resemble the biographies of so many artists of the 19th Century which are an abrupt catastrophic break with bourgeois family tradition. In 1854, at twenty years of age, after attending the Lycée Louis-le-Grand, and brief studies at the Ecole de Doit, Edgar became the pupil of an insignificant disciple of Ingres, Louis Lamothe, who cultivated an academic, eclectic, bloodless style in the David tradition, devoid of any revolutionary pathos. This period of instruction, and also his short stay at the Ecole des Beaux-Arts in 1855, had no immediate and practical effect on his work. Nevertheless this period had its importance for Degas, because at that time he developed a profound admiration for Ingres, which lasted throughout his life. To Degas, Lamothe was only the medium through which he had a glimpse of the art of his revered master. It was through the art-collector, Valpinçon, that Degas made the acquaintance of Ingres. On their first meeting, Ingres gave him the advice which Degas later quotes: « Draw lines, plenty of lines whether from memory or according to nature ». This advice remained a precious legacy for him and is a maxim which could be written as a motto over all his artistic achievements.

His apprenticeship to Lamothe and work at the Ecole des Beaux-Arts might quite easily have interfered with, or even arrested any natural development of his artistic powers. This considerable danger Degas, however, escaped by visiting the Louvre as often as possible and studying and copying the old masters, particularly the Italian painters of the 15th Century. In 1856, Degas travelled for the first time to Italy, where he intended to make the acquaintance of his Italian relatives. This journey, which is followed by another in 1858, and several more in 1859 — with long, productive stays in Naples, Rome, Florence, and Umbria — was most valuable for Degas' final growth as an artist. The study of the old masters, which had already begun in the Louvre and in the Cabinet des Estampes, now found a systematic continuation. However, it was not the masters of the High Renaissance, headed by Raphael, who made the strongest impression on Degas; as might have been expected of a pupil of Lamothe's and the Ecole des Beaux-Arts, he preferred the painters of the 15th Century, such as Uccello, Benozzo Gozzoli, Ghirlandajo, Mantegna, Signorelli, Perugino, Lorenzo di Credi, and those exponents of Florentine Mannerism, Pontormo and Bronzino. Degas had, of course, already drawn in the Louvre, and also in Italy, using Leonardo, Michelangelo and Raphael as models, but the highly accentuated idealism of Classicism remained foreign to him. This was especially so, since the David school had demonstrated to a shocking degree how quickly imitation of the classical form results in flat and empty virtuosity.

If one asks the reason for Degas' preference for the 15th Century painting, it must be answered that it is here that he saw most clearly realized, in the painting of the past, his idea of the reality and artistic truth of the words Ingres is supposed to have said about the works of Raphael in comparing them to the work of David's followers; « How they have disappointed me ». Degas could have said the same in a different context, when, in Italy, he confessed to his choice.

His turning to the Italian « Primitives » — the definition which was used far into the 20th Century, originated at the beginning of the 19th Century in France as well as in Germany ([4]) — is not an isolated

4) ANDRÉ CHASTEL, *Le goût des « Préraphaélites » en France,* in: De Giotto à Bellini, Exhibition at the Orangerie des Tuileries, Paris 1956, Foreword to the Catalogue, p. VII ff.

case. As to France, the Barbus sect, gathering round Maurice Quai, a pupil of David's, had formed an independent group which opposed static, dying Classicism. They saw their salvation in the return to the « Primitive ». For them, this primitive art manifested itself most clearly in the rather vague formula of « prephidiac art ». The Barbus group soon received European recognition for their anticlassical arguments, which consisted in the abstraction of lines and derived largely from a literary concept. The German Lukasbruder or Nazarener joined forces in 1808, as did the young French painters around 1830. The painting of the Italian and German « Primitives » set the pattern for their ideas. The movement reached its zenith in 1848 with the English Pre-Raphaelite fraternity, which was completely opposed to « the sentiment of the schools of the Renaissance, composed of idleness, infidelity, sensuality, and frivolous pride ». They raved enthusiastically about the art of the « Primitives » as a superior stage in the realm of holiness, and attributed to it an almost ritual quality, believing thus to escape modern vulgarity.

Nineteenth Century Pre-Raphaelism, be it the German, French or English form of expression, held no fascination for Degas. He did not take part in the development of the religious art of Classicism (which led from Ingres to Puvis de Chavannes and Maurice Denis), because his assimilation of the « Primitives » transcends all other interpretations. Degas' early work within 19th Century art, bears witness to the fact that a painter can, on the other hand, hark back to a great extent to long past forms of arts, while, at the same time participating in contemporary art, and, on the other hand, through this very process, create a strictly personal and unmistakable form.

At the beginning of Degas' artistic activity we also have copies and studies of old masters whose works he came to know at the Louvre and in Italy. After this, he painted types, especially women of the working classes, art studies bordering on the *genre pittorisque* such as, for example, Léopold Robert and the German Nazarener had successfully cultivated. For Degas, however, this was only an episode.

For the first time, the art of the young painter achieves an authentic ring in the field of portrait-painting, where knowledge drawn from the old art is combined with an individual mastery. The people Degas depicts are almost all members of his family, especially sisters and brothers, and, above all, himself. He painted about one and a half dozen self-portraits, mainly in his early period; later, Degas no longer felt compelled to occupy himself with his own person. This tendency therefore disappears, and gives way to a more general, objective form of creative purpose. Of his self-portraits, the one painted in 1854-55 is among the most perfect and representative. It shows most faithfully how the twenty-year-old Degas wanted to be seen and how he understood himself at that time. On a neutral background the half-length portrait of the painter appears behind a balustrade with his bent arm leaning against it, in a classical pose which had been used over and over again since Durer's self-portrait in 1498 (Prado, Madrid), and Raphael's portrait of Angelo Doni in about 1506 (Palazzo Pitti, Florence). The European style of portrait demanded that the model should not be shown in a spontaneous or idle position, but rather solemnly represented in an attitude of elegant aloofness. This Degas achieves to an unsurpassed degree in his self-portrait. The artist is not an exponent of the carefree, daring world of the Bohemian but a distinguished and serious-minded citizen. The high, narrow shape of the canvas and area chosen cause the top of the head almost to touch the upper rim of the picture. The face has a distant, enraptured expression, the eyes are half-closed and have an absent look. It is that spiritual expression which, like a delicate halo, permeates the subjects painted by the Mannerists, from Pontormo to Bronzino.

Portrait of a Woman. Pencil. Gallery Wildenstein, Paris - New York.

Study for the "Femme aux Chrysanthèmes". Pencil. Paul J. Sachs Collection.

THE BELLELLI FAMILY. Oil, 1860. (80" × 101"),
The Louvre Museum, Paris

PORTRAIT OF JAMES TISSOT. Oil, c. 1868. (24" × 17½"),
Metropolitan Museum of Art, New York

PORTRAIT OF MADAME CAMUS AT THE PIANO.
Oil, 1869. (56" × 37½"), ▷
Emil G. Buehrle Collection, Zurich

POUTING. Oil, 1868. (13" × 19"),
Metropolitan Museum of Art, New York

PORTRAIT OF MADEMOISELLE DIHAU AT THE PIANO. Oil, 1868. (16"×13"),
The Louvre Museum, Paris ▷

PORTRAIT OF A WOMAN WITH RED SHAWL. 1886. (30″ × 25″), Collection Emil G. Buehrle, Zurich

Portrait of Walter Sickert, Daniel Halevy, Ludovic Halevy, J. E. Blanche, Gerves and Boulanger Cave. Pastel.

Degas' early portraits achieve their culmination in a work which crowns 19th Century portrait-painting; the « Bellelli Family ». This depicts Laura de Gas, Edgar's aunt, her husband, Baron Bellelli, who was an Italian Senator and a friend of Cavour — and their children Jeanne and Julie. Degas occupied himself with this group painting for years. The first sketches were done in 1856 in Naples, and others, from 1857 to 1860, in Florence, where the Bellelli family lived. The painting was probably begun in 1857, but not finished before 1862 in Paris. Degas was thinking of exhibiting it in the Paris « Salon » an intention, however, which was never fulfilled. In the « Salon », this picture, which remained in his studio until his death, would undoubtedly have created a scandal — and Degas had to avoid this for the sake of the illustrious Bellelli family. Today, it seems inconceivable that this fear of scandal could apply to a work which has become to be looked upon as the epitome of portrait-painting according to the classical concept. However, this would not be thinking in historical terms; in fact, this painting was considered at the time, to be of revolutionary boldness when compared to the officially-accepted concept of portrait-painting, for which photographic fidelity and conventional « snapshot » pose, were the indispensable conditions. With Degas, the figures do not pose solely for the viewer as they do in contemporary photographs, and in the portraits which came under their influence and were accepted by the « Salon »; only Jeanne, one of the daughters, looks out of the picture towards an imaginary object in front of her. The others are shown simply as they are; the Baroness looks proud and erect, and has a rigid, severe deportment. The black of her garments (she was in mourning in 1862 for her son, Jean, who had died young) underlines the impression of noble reserve. Little Julie is caught at a moment of transitory movement; she sits on the arm of a chair and her left leg is crossed under her — a liberty meant to express a spontaneous directness which must have appeared to the academic painting of the time a veritable sacrilege. Even less does the figure of the Baron show any hint of official pose. Seen half from behind, it is turned to one side in the armchair; only the movement·of the head brings it into relationship with the other persons, while his head is actually directed toward the paper on the table. The Baron is completely enshrined in this homely, intimate, informal atmosphere. This way of Degas of seeing a picture was later to catch his models in an aimless, detached pose and here we see it for the first time.

These deviations from the academic concept in favour of a « true life » directness, of a « slice of life » also distinguished Degas' « Bellelli Family » from the only comparable examples of similar type among Ingres' group sketches. On the other hand, his painting obeys a set of rules in its formal structure, which adheres strictly to truly architectural. The clarity with which the figures, particularly of the women and the two children, emerge in pyramidical precision before the wall of the room, set parallel at the back of the picture — against which they are framed and encircled by a system of right-angles, which densify the main direction of the planes — is closely related to the painting of Florentine Mannerism, particularly the Medici portrait by Bronzino. The black, grey, and white of the clothes underline, together with the precise drawing, the severity of the concept. Only in the colours of the surroundings — the delicate blue of the tapestry pattern, the greyish yellow of the spot carpet, the gold of the frame — is there a merging into atmospherical softness, a quality of translucence — and the mirror above the fireplace gives the room an illusory, yet charming note. The « Bellelli Family » is Degas' first entirely personal artistic achievement. It holds a memorable place in 19th Century group painting. Group paintings representing corporate bodies, or heads of social clubs — a kind of painting that reached its peak in the Baroque era, especially in Holland — no longer existed in the 19th Century

Portrait of Manet. Pen and ink.

— at least none of any notable artistic value, except perhaps for the artists of that period who portrayed themselves in groups. To this class belong some French paintings, Fantin-Latours' composition « Homage to Delacroix » (1864) and « Manet's Studio » (1865), both of which are, however, in the category of the photographically-posed, « living » pictures. Only the individual's family ties still merited genuine artistic application, since no other ties possessed the organic strength to be considered worthwhile painting (⁵). Those painters of the first half of the 19th Century, for whom the family portraits still had any importance — for example, Ingres in France, Runge in Germany, and Waldmüller and Amerling in Austria — renounced the attitude of the 18th Century. The 18th Century is characterised to such an extent by an overwhelming feeling for happy family life, for the harmony of couples, for home-life and its filial joys that one can rightly call these works: « devotion paintings ». Now, in the 19th Century it was primarily bourgeois dignity, often verging on antiquated rigidity, and representing moral servity, that predominated, although it was gradually declining. It was replaced by an extreme informality of grouping, in which inner bearing, the order and closeness of the concept of « family » are assailed by doubts. This stage is reached in Rayskis' picture of the « Chamberlain von Schroeter and His Family », on the steps outside Biederstein Castle, and it is expressed to a high degree by Degas himself in his « Place de la Concorde » (1874-75), which, although it has as its theme a family picture — the Viscount Lepic with his daughters — makes the public square the real subject of the painting; here, the persons depicted appear only as passers-by, and are subordinated to chance and whim. Viewed from this angle, the « Bellelli Family » has only now achieved its particular importance in Degas' work and in 19th Century painting. Far removed as it is from the prettiness of the early Victorian style and from the photographical pose, this painting once more represents the concept of the family, an institution depending on dignity, morality, and responsibility. In it, however, can be felt a trace of cool distance which leaves no room for the intimate expression that triumphs in « Place de la Concorde ». The work draws its significance and its greatness from spiritual tension and its formal, artistic mastery.

At the heart of the work of the young Degas, there can be found, apart from the portrait, the religious and the historical painting with mythological themes. This does not come about accidentally. To the classical doctrine of art which leads far into the 19th Century, historical subjects seemed the most dignified and highest kind of painting, a kind of painting suited to take over the legitimate function exercised by religious art up to the destruction of the artistic tradition of Western Christianity in the French Revolution. In order to illustrate this situation, it is perhaps sufficient to recall, Friedrich Theodor Vischer's remark about « history... a field for the modern artist » in his « Paths of Criticism » in 1844. A young painter in Paris around 1860, whose ambition it was to exhibit in the « Salon », could not help turning to historical painting, and Degas did this between 1860 and 1865 with five compositions of which numerous sketches and several final versions exist; « Young Spartans Exercising » (1860); « The Building of a Town by Semiramis » (1861); « Alexander and Bucephalus » 1861-62); « The Daughter of Jephtah » (1861-64); « The Suffering of the Town of Orleans » (1865), the last named being accepted for the 1865 « Salon ».

These works have been criticized unjustly, for they are paintings of a strong character which are unequalled in the whole of 19th Century Historian Painting. Degas draws from many different sources —

5) Hermann Beeken, *19th* Century German Art, Munich 1944 p. 388.

The Foyer de la Danse at the Rue le Peletier Opera. Oil, 1872. ($12\frac{1}{2}'' \times 19''$), The Louvre Museum, Paris

PORTRAIT OF ROSE ADELAIDE DE GAS. Oil, 1870. (11" × 9"), The Louvre Museum, Paris

PORTRAIT OF A WOMAN WITH A VASE OF FLOWERS. Oil, 1872. (26" × 22"), The Louvre Museum, Paris

THE COTTON MARKET IN NEW ORLEANS. Oil, 1873. (30" × 37"), Museum of Art, Pau, France

in the case of « Alexander and Bucephalus » and the « Young Spartans » it is Plutarch ([6]) — but both concept and style are clear and uniform. Figurine groups appear in a kind of bas-relief before wide landscapes, in such a way that there exists between the figures and the landscape a strange lack of relationship — a characteristic of the Florentine 15th Century. There is no apparent connection between figures and surroundings, and even among themselves, the figures are hardly connected by related movement. On the whole, the groups have the character of artificial pose. The myth-creating power of the imagination, which reached far into the 18th Century up to the time of Tiepolo and the painters of the later German Baroque era, and which were able to inject into religious and mythological work some genuine, exuberant life, was obliterated by overpowering meditative thought, which became the inevitable fate of Classicism in all its expressions.

It is all the more surprising that Degas succeeded in depicting the figures each in their own particular individuality, with startlingly intense vitality — and this because he transferred them direct from his sketchbook on to the canvas. In this way they express convincing mirth as studies of life and movement. In this, and also in the wonderful freshness of the warm colours, especially of the landscape-backgrounds, lies the « promise for the future ». For the otherwise strictly classical compositions, all Degas had to do was to replace the antiquated figure foreground scenery by an original design of his own in order to provide the path along which his talent could develop.

« The Daughter of Jephtah » shows, however, that Degas' history-painting cannot be considered in the same light. This picture is the most mature and perfect example of all his historical paintings. Judging by its size — the painting measures almost $78^6/_8$" $\times$ $118^1/_8$" — it is the largest canvas Degas ever painted, which indicates that the artist has arrived at some sort of total of conclusions regarding his endeavours in the field of historical painting ([7]). A scene from the Old Testament is represented: the gileadith Jephtah has vowed that if he defeats the Ammanites, he will bring, as a sacrifice to Jahven, the first living creature he meets on his return, and, fate ordained that it was his own daughter (Book of Judges Chapter 2, Verse 30). Although Degas is moved in this painting by manifold inspiration, the composition goes back to a painting of the Sienese, Girolamo Genga, to Cesare da Sestas, « Worship of the Kings » and to Poussin's « Rape of the Sabines ». The group of young women reflects Botticelli's style; to the right, with his back turned. the figure of the soldier is reminiscent of Mantegna, while Jephtah on horseback reminds one of Delacroix. Nevertheless, a compelling, formal and atmospheric unity is achieved in the dramatic movement that pulses through this great work of art. The design is no longer parallel to the picture, but brought into a complex dimensional form. Degas occasionally felt affinity to Delacroix, at times wavering between « the commandments of his master Ingres and the strange magic of Delacroix » (Valérey), and it was in his « Daughter of Jephtah » that he came nearest of all to Delacroix's romanticism. In one of his studies Degas made colour-notes, which demonstrate with what care and conscious forethought he also developed his colour-scene: Colour was never for him a medium for expressing irrational impulsive movement, least of all in his ears. « A grey-blue sky so effective that the bright lights stand out and the shadow emerges naturally as black. For

6) The latter theme was perhaps conveyed to Degas by he book « Voyage du Jeune Anacharsis en Grèce » by the Abbé Barthélémy. The Italian painter, Giovanni Demin, had also painted a fresco in 1856 on the same subject in Villa Patti, near Sedico, and Delacroix used it to make a sketch for a fresco intended for the Palais Bourbon, which finally, however, was not used. Degas must have been acquainted with both works.

7) Compare with Eleanor Mitchell's analysis « The Daughter of Jephtah by Degas, genesis, evolution » in: Gazette des Beaux-Arts, 1937, II, p. 175-189.

Dancers at the Bar, Study. Gouache and Watercolour.

the red of Jephtah's robe, remember the reddish-orange shades used for the old man in Delacroix's...,
The hill with all its dull patches and bluish greens Omit much, sketch landscape in vaguely. Some
heads raised and « lit up » in profile behind Jephtah; greyish pea-green with off-white, striped belt and
blue veil with pinkish tints » ([8]).

The romantic undercurrent in « The Daughter of Jephtah » re-appears, even more accentuated, in the
painting of « Mlle. Fiocre in the ballet "La Source" », painted shortly afterwards. The theme, of course,
concerns the world of the theatre — Eugenie Fiocre was a dancer at the Opera, and one of her main
successes was Leo Delibe's ballet, "La Source". This first theatrical painting by Degas strikes us rather
as the portrayal of a bewilderingly exotic, oriental scene, filled with magic. The theatrical element here
is not taken from the reality of the stage as in Degas' later paintings of the theatre, but appears as an
element of generally romantic, unrealistic and fantastic quality. And yet we must not overlook that
in each particular — like the drinking horse — a « realistic » vision expresses itself; this is no longer
the romantic « battle-horse » of the Jephtah picture but a real live study. It was no accident that Degas
later sculptured this horse in clay.

What manifests itself in a detail like this of a completely romantic work like « La Source » is, however,
a symptom that demands our serious attention, because, in the later 60's there took place the great
« turning-point » in Degas' work, the change from historical painting to his determined and conscious
conflict with his own epoch. The reasons for this switch are primarily to be found within Degas himself; he begins now to create according to his true artistic temperament, which had in a way been
held in subjection till then by doctrinal considerations. Besides this, there are other, external reasons
for this change that must not be passed over lightly.

A decisive factor here was his acquaintance with Manet, for it was through the painter of « Dejeuner
sur l'herbe » and the « Olympia » — paintings which laid the foundations of a new aestheticism — that
Degas came into contact with Monet, Pissarro, Renoir, Bazille and Cézanne, all of whom admired
Manet as the leader of a new art. These artists would meet in the Café Guerbois, in the Grande rue des
Batignolles (now Av. de Clichy), and the circle was enlarged by the engravers Bracquemond and Desboutin, the painter Fantin-Latour, Guillemet, Stevens, the draughtsman Constantin Guys, and the
writers Astruc, Duranty, Burty, Zola and Duret. As early as 1845, at the end of his report on the
« Salon » of that year, Baudelaire spoke of the « heroism of modern life » and wrote the famous sentence: « the real painter will be he who will be able to extract from present-day life its epic quality,
thus enabling us to see and understand, by means of colour or drawing, how great and poetical we are
in our ties and sparkling boots »; and a year later, in the « Salon » report for the year 1846, he said:
« Parisian life is rich in marvellously poetical subjects. That which is marvellous envelops and refreshes
us like the atmosphere, and we won't believe it ». Similar remarks and principles expounded by Baudelaire now entered the circle at the Café Guerbois, and, with it, the realm of immediate realization.
That which had shown — at first very reluctantly — in the landscape-painting of Corot, Rousseau,
Chintreuil, Français, Flers, Daubigny, Harpignies and Cassatt, who presented the unobtrusive subject
of free landscape as opposed to metropolitan life, now became the central idea of a new art concept.
This was the interpretation of the immediate present, and Degas assimilated this thought through the
mediation of Duranty, whose thoughts had the same naturally sharp, clear-sightedness. Although Du-

8) PAUL-ANDRÉ LEMOISNE, *Degas et Son Oeuvre*, Paris 1954, p. 45.

Study of a Dancing Girl. Gouache.

THE REHEARSAL. Oil, 1873. (27" × 22"), Dumbarton Oaks Collection, Washington, D.C.

CAFÉ-CHANTANT. Pastel on paper. ($9^1/_4$" × $16^3/_4$"),
Corcoran Gallery of Art, Washington, D.C.

Café-Concert (« Les Ambassadeurs »). Pastel on monotype. 1876. (12½″ × 10″), Museum of Art, Lyon, France

CAFÉ-CONCERT: « THE SONG OF THE DOG ». Gouache and pastel on paper, 1877. (17¹/₄" × 15¹/₂"),
Coll. Horace Havemeyer Jr., New York

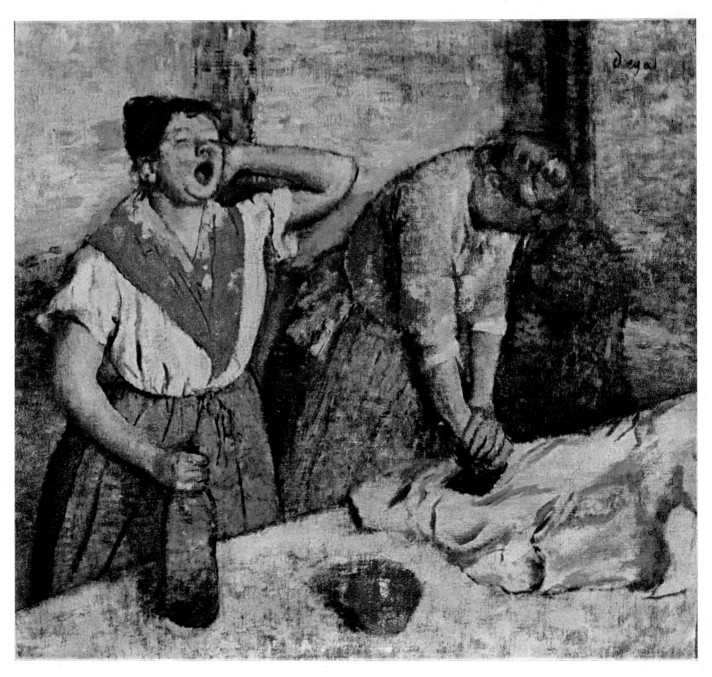

Two Laundresses. Pastel on canvas, about 1884. (30" × 32¼"),
The Louvre Museum, Paris

◁ L'Absinthe (Portraits of Ellen Andrée and Marcellin Desboutin).
Oil, 1877. (37" × 27½), The Louvre Museum, Paris

39

INTERIOR (THE RAPE). Oil 1874. (81″ × 116″). Coll. H. P. McIlhenny, Philadelphia

ranty's paper, *Le Réalisme,* which appeared in 1856, soon afterwards disappeared again, his ideas, which revolved round the present and contemporary life, and its adequate artistic realization, continued to ferment. « How can it be that we are less interesting than our predecessors? Why have painters not followed literature, or have they adopted only romantic extravagances? » ([9]). Those are the questions Duranty asks again and again. Later on, after 1865, Degas was in full accord with the ideas of Duranty, both as regards theory and in his practical artistic activity. Finally, it was his art which Duranty referred to, when he summed up attitudes and problems in 1876 in the pamphlet *La Nouvelle Peinture.* « Let us take leave of the stylized human body, which is treated like a vase. What we need is the characteristic modern person — in his clothes, in the midst of his social surroundings, at home or out in the street... The observation of his home life and such peculiarities as his profession creates in him. A person with a back..., which shows us a temperament, an age, a social condition... people and things, as they present themselves in a million ways and involuntarily in real life ». Apart from Duranty, only the brothers Edmond and Jules de Goncourt, among the temporary authors, had a similarly strong influence on Degas especially with their novel *Manette Salomon* which appeared in 1866. The central figure of this novel is an artist, who lives in the middle of the 19th Century. The Goncourts also demand that the artist should have the right to portray modern existence and the new themes and motifs which Paris can offer. In 1874, Edmond de Goncourt visited Degas, he was already able to see how much Degas' art was in accordance with his opinions on modern art: « So far, of all the men I have seen, he has been the one who has best caught the atmosphere of modern life and the spirit of the present » ([9a]).

Under the influence of this idea, Degas' art underwent a complete change between the years 1865 and 1870. However, this change took place very gradually in his portrait-painting. And yet portraits of that period, conventional as they are, are distinguished by a tendency toward the character-drawing and the portrayal of the unique quality of face and deportment. Their roots go back to the heritage of the psychological portraitists who reach their peak with Corneille de Lyon, Clouet, Holbein and the Florentine Mannerists. Among the most important of these portraits are those of the Duchess of Morbilli (1863), of the two sisters of Mme. Ganjelin, of a student of the Polytechnic, Mlle. Dobigny, Mme. Hertel, the « Young Girls at the Piano », « Degas and Valernes » (around 1864), Mlle. Helène Hertel (1865), « The Woman with the Chrysanthemums » (1865), Rose-Adelaide Degas (1867), « The Amateur » (1866), Hortense Valpinçon (1869), Henry Valpinçon (1870), « Portrait of James Tissot » (1868), « The Guitarist Pagans and Mr. Degas » (about 1869), « Mme. Camus at the Piano » (about 1869). Degas himself theorises: « To create in the head the expression (in the academic style) of a study in modern sentiment... Beauty must only be represented by a certain type of face... One must paint portraits of people in typical and familiar attitudes and, above all, give to their faces the same expression as one gives their bodies. Thus, if a person is the laughing type, make him laugh » ([10]).

Although people are caught in their casual poses, in spontaneous moods reflecting a natural charm, serene, formal behaviour sometimes breaks through nonetheless. The painting of Mme. Camus at the

9) LEMOISNE, p. 48.
9a) *Journal des Goncourts* V (1872-1877), Paris 1931, p. 112.
10) LEMOISNE, p. 52

Study for the painting "The Dancing Class". Charcoal.

Study of a Dancing Girl. Pencil.

STUDY OF THREE DANCING GIRLS. Charcoal, about 1888.
Bibliothéque Donat, Paris.

44

GIRLS COMBING THEIR HAIR. Oil on paper, 1876. ($12^{1}/_{4}$" × $17^{3}/_{4}$"),
Duncan Phillips Memorial Gallery, Washington, D.C.

AT THE RACES (AMATEUR JOCKEYS). Oil, 1879. (26" × 32"),
The Louvre Museum, Paris

JOCKEYS. Oil, About 1885. ($10^1/_4$" $\times$ $15^3/_8$"),
Yale University Art Gallery, New Haven, Conn.

MISS LALA AT THE
FERNANDO CIRCUS.
Oil, 1879.
(53" × 30"),
National Gallery,
London

piano — the subject was the wife of the Japanese enthusiast, Doctor Camus, a friend of Degas' and Manet's, and she had an excellent reputation as a pianist — is touched by a last wave of Ingrisme, and it bears witness at the same time to his closeness to Manet in its cultivated elegance. He places the figure against its background and in space by means of a rhomboid frame. The picture, composed of several objects, strikes a balance between a « professional » portrait and an absolutely representative portrait. Each detail of the costume and the surroundings — down to the incredibly delicate china-figure, which throws a light shadow against the wall and the mirror with its precious, colourful frame — is designed to draw attention to the woman: it indicates her personality, which is full of culture, elegance and grace; it reveals in the expression of her smiling face a tender tranquility. It is thus simply the harmony of the human figure with the way it is dressed, and the things around it, that expresses the world the woman has created, the sum-total of the personality portrayed.

More radically than in the portrait, which in its definition remains fundamentally strongly bound to tradition, Degas has been able to realize his artistic intentions through the choice of new themes: he creates something like a new iconography which now consequently finds its place in contemporary life. His most important pictures deal with jockeys, race courses, Ballet and the Stage, Cafés Chantants with their fortune-tellers, and, finally, the slum world: the workmen, washer-women and milliners.

Horse-racing, a sport of English origin, did not become popular on the Continent until the end of the 18th Century, and soon it was also the subject of paintings by Carle Vernet and, afterwards, by Séricault, who were both inspired by English works. In the fiction of the 19th Century, from Balzac to Tolstoy, horse-racing played an important part, and as a matter of course, painters also become interested in this theme which was so important a part of society. Manet pointed out the elegant social aspects of it, while Degas showed keen observation of the moving body of the animal. What was movement of light and atmosphere for the Impressionists became the movement of the animal — or human body — for Degas. His earliest interest in the race course as a subject dates back to the beginning of the sixties. Degas' main interest is in the Jockeys — but his searching eye often depicts the world of the onlookers as well. This brings about such charming results as « La voiture aux courses » (1870-73), where the carriage is boldly put into the lower right-hand corner of the picture and is partly outside the picture. This gives the theme a documentary vividness and reality. The people in the carriage are caught in their fashionable elegance. Furthermore, the relationship between the women and the child seems to bring out that tender intimacy which was to influence Vuillard. The carriage in the foreground contrasts with the wide space in which the race is being run; the perspective is given by the riders at different distances and by a second carriage. The cool green of the spring landscape and the tones of the sky blending into a bluish-grey are quite different from the atmospheric effects with which Monet was experimenting at that particular time. It is much more the noble, subtle, Corot-like harmony of colour which, in addition to its strong design, gives to the painting its wonderfully clear character.

In constantly new attempts Degas varies the theme of the race track. On the 27th of September, 1881, when the newspaper *Le Globe* reproduced the Englishman, Major Muybridge's snapshots showing particular phases of a galloping horse, Degas made use of them as a guide in his movement studies. It became evident that the way in which galloping horses were depicted in English engravings, with their front legs outstretched, was faulty. But this is how Degas portrays his race-horses in the painting « La voiture aux courses ». The painting « Avant les courses » (painted 1878-80) is an

After the Bath. Charcoal.

Dancing Girl Pulling Her Stocking. Gouache.

Study of a Dancing Girl. Charcoal.

REPOSE. Pastel on paper, about 1893. (19$\frac{1}{4}$" × 25$\frac{1}{2}$"),
Former Collection Sam Lewisohn, New York

THE MILLINERY SHOP. Oil, 1882. ($32^7/_8$" × $42^7/_8$"),
The Art Institute of Chicago, Illinois

54

example of those works which epitomize the fleeting moment of the movement. The asymmetry of the composition and the planal structure of the design agree with Degas' desire to achieve the effect of actual movement. « Aux course: Jockeys amateurs près d'une voiture » is closely related compositionally to « La voiture aux course ». Each time the emphasis lies off centre in the lower right-hand part of the painting, cut off by the corner of the frame. But instead of a « naturalistic » treatment of form, colour now dominates, laid on in broad patches. As before, Degas is attracted by the nervousness and elegance, the disciplined dancing grace of the horses; but all the details merge into the harmony of colour values, which keep the plane covered like a mosaic: people, animals and landscape are combined to give an ornamental, planal and extremely decorative effect; here the principles of creation which will dominate in his later years can already be seen.

In the autumn of 1872, Degas travelled to the U.S.A. in the company of his brother, René, in order to visit two brothers in New Orleans (the birthplace of his mother), where they were living as cotton-traders. The journey was very welcome to the painter, as the Franco-Prussian War, in which he had been called up for the Infantry during the siege of Paris, meant an unwelcome interruption in his life. Degas was not the only one who felt a desire to leave France for a certain time — Duret, Manet, Berthe Morisot and Monet had also gone abroad in these post-war years. His stay in the New World lasted till April 1873. Degas was highly impressed by the alien exotic « colonial » surroundings; his numerous letters are evidence of this. But on the whole, he realized that he needed Paris in order to be able to create. He felt that only the things familiar to him, through ingrained habit, were able to inspire him. « I want only my own corner and to devote myself to it. Art does not expand, but repeats itself. If you must needs have a comparison, let me tell you that, in order to produce good fruit, you must grow it on a trellis. We stand there all our lives our arms outstretched and our mouths open, in order to catch anything that passes by or that surrounds us, and to live by it » ([11]). So the artistic result of the journey was poor. Apart from the portraits of his relatives, only one of his masterpieces is due to his American stay, and this was the first painting, incidentally, to be bought by a museum (in 1878, by the town of Pau): the « Cotton Exchange in New Orleans ». This picture represents quite a complex new formulation of the group portrait as well as its interior background. In front, wearing a top-hat and testing cotton samples, sits Mr. Musson, the artist's uncle; behind, appears René de Gas, with an open newspaper, while the other brother, Achille de Gas, leans on a window sill on the left. The problem of reproducing contemporary material, an account of informal everyday business activity, has here been brilliantly solved by Degas. The room in the factory has an impersonal sobriety and coolness, an economical restraint which, later, was also the case with the *salles* of the ballet-dancers. The desire to impersonalize the interior goes so far that it takes on some of the aspects of the public square the figures of the clients and salesmen, the clerks and accountants stand, or walk about, or sit almost haphazardly. The colours are muted; dull browns, grays and ochres predominate. The greatness of this picture perhaps lies in the way realistic and vivid movement is sketched almost photographically but with a clarity and life that are far beyond anything a camera can do. « The Cotton Exchange » is one of Degas' most magnificent works in his « naturalistic » period. It is comparable to his work during his greatest period, which lasted from 1873-1886.

11) *Lettres de Degas* (to Frolich, 27 Nov. 1872), Paris 1931, p. 4.

THE TUB. Pastel on paper,
◁ 1886. (23⅝" × 32⅝"),
The Louvre, Paris

How a great painter, for whom the horse and the sporting world of the turf could provide the source for one side of his vision, could then turn towards the Theatre, the Stage and the Ballet with yet greater insistence and intensity of concentration, may well puzzle the merely superficial observer, but these seemingly so different themes have one vital quality in common: movement. Horses, like ballerinas, are both exquisite and highly trained creatures of movement. Through them it was possible for Degas to express one of his inner urges: the movement of the body — through the eyes of Degas. Paul Valéry was able to combine horse and ballerina in an almost coquettish way: « The horse walks on tiptoe. Four hoofs support him. No animal has in it the poise of the prima ballerina like a thoroughbred when perfectly balanced. »

This obsession with the theatre is in Degas' blood. In his Theatre, Stage and Ballet painting he conquered a new realm for art, for these paintings differ profoundly from the theatrical painting which we know in the art of the 18th Century. The greatest painter of the Rococo period, Watteau, was inspired by the figures of the Commedia dell'Arte, and used them to paint pictures that made the world of the stage accepted as a means of expression for the very highest of aesthetic ideals. Eventually, with him, though more so with his successors, it became just an excuse for frivolous gaiety and nothing more. Watteau and Tiepolo paint the figures of the comedy isolated; with him, they become transformed too much into the melancholy symbols of human existence. Degas, however, turns his ruthless attention to the stage for its own sake — and this to a growing degree as the eye sees things — and tends more and more to express what he sees there in terms of what the eye can see and hold in a moment of time — a fleeting « snapshot ». Degas' first theatrical paintings are portraits — which does not surprise us. Actually, the earliest work which concerns the world of the theatre, « Mlle. Fiocre in the Ballet 'La Source'», is nothing but the portrait of a ballerina while she is dancing. Between 1868 and 1869, Degas painted the picture « l'Orchestre de l'Operà ». In it he portrays a number of musicians, among them the composer, Chabrier, the flautist, Atlès, the violinist, Lancien, the bassoonist, Gouffé, and last but not least the bassoonist, Dilian; most of these were friends of Degas. We again see put into practice in this picture, which is one among many paintings and studies of this subject, an extreme example of this concept of an informal portrait of people surrounded by the instruments and objects which go to make up their professional world.

After his return from America, Degas plunged with ardent zeal into the world he had missed so much for so long. He now takes a very important step forward: he no longer only depicts what the audience or musicians can see of the stage, but goes, as a cool, sober observer, behind the stage in order to watch the ballerinas at their rehearsals. The theatre changes from merely being the incidental setting of his picture, to becoming the sole centre of interest in it, and the whole of the world it portrays. In the paintings « The Foyer de la Danse » at the Rue de Peletier Opera (1872) and « Classe de Danse » the ballerinas appear at the rehearsal in rooms which the eye really penetrates; they are not described symmetrically. We always see them from an unusual angle, and only partially. They create the stark, unadorned scene of the demanding, stylized, almost ritual exercises performed by the young devotees of dancing. The girls stand along the walls, listening to the ballet-master and the violinist. They are graceful and flower-like. He paints them as cupolas and domes of silk, yet they are caught with a fanatical sense of reality as they go through their exacting movements and exercises, which range from careless repose to high tension. The arrangement of the figures in the

WOMAN BATHING. Charcoal.

59

Dancer Fixing Her Shoulder-Strap. Gouache.

DANCERS. Pastel on cardboard, 1899. (24" × 25$\frac{1}{8}$"),
Toledo Museum of Art, Ohio

PIERROT AND PIERRETTE.   BALLET SCENE. 1887.
Private Collection

◁ A BALLET SCENE FROM AN OPERA BOX. Pastel on paper, 1885. (25¹⁄₈" × 19¹⁄₄"),
Museum of Art, Philadelphia

63

THE CLOSE OF AN
ARABESQUE.
Pastel and oil,
about 1880.
(26" × 14$\frac{1}{2}$"),
The Louvre Museum,
Paris

Study of a Dancing Girl. Charcoal.

Study of a Dancing Girl. Gouache.

room is carried out with utmost precision; chairs desks and other objects are rhythmically related to the human figures. Degas is a master of tension, the intense atmosphere of the room: he makes the room's very emptiness ring. This nobody else has been able to recognize so well as Liebermann, who says about Degas: « Not only does he arrange the room, but he uses the room itself as a medium for creating. The distance of one object from another often determines the composition » ([12]).

Degas painted all his ballet pictures in his studio from sketches which he made during dancing lessons. In this respect, too, he differs clearly from the Impressionists; he observes without painting, and he paints without observation ([13]). Then, after works which show the rehearsal-hall or the stage, even if we only see a part of them as a static pictorial unit, astounding variations of the same motive were achieved through the unorthodox way their subjects were treated by this painter. He changes the angle at which he sees them to his liking, so that the dancers are presented in the most surprising positions. More and more they are painted from close-up, singly or in groups; without the three-dimensional room around them, they fill the foreground with areas of colour, in front of the wings and curtains. One must acknowledge the greatness of the various versions of the « Danseuse au bouquet, saluant sur la scène » (around 1877-78). As a Sylphe, whose body does not seem to be flesh and bone, the ballerina, at the close of her graceful solo, with her arms outstretched in acknowledgement of the audience's applause, is shown in a brilliant spotlight with the unreal, fantastic, décor of the ballet as her background. She gives expression to the words of a sonnet by Degas himself: « *Equilibre, balance et ton vol et ton poids.* »

The downy lightness of her message to the audience is only seemingly pure Impressionism. It has been achieved through infinitely patient and accurate observation in the form of sketches and notes. Degas himself has emphasized this fact in his art in the following sentence: « No art is less spontaneous than mine. What I do is the result of thinking and the study of the great masters. I know nothing about such things as inspiration, spontaneity, and temperament. » And finally: « One has to repeat the same thing ten, or rather a hundred times. In art nothing must be left to accident — not even movement. »

His later paintings of dancers remove the figures completely from the realistic atmosphere of the rehearsal room. The glittering tracery of colours, like fire-works, now reigns supreme; and this makes it possible for the figures to become pure emanations of the colour with no life outside the picture, with no individuality or personality of their own. They are completely engulfed by the rhythm of frozen movement. The dance is no longer a performance that requires arduous hours of practice before it can be mastered, nor an ordinary expression of life. It is no longer only a conscious, and therefore superficial, expression of beauty; it is now a ritual and active embodiment of a real myth.

Between 1875 and 1880, Degas frequently visited « Café-Concerts ». These places, where the pulse of the Metropolis, its everyday life, could be felt as it could nowhere else, fascinated him. The pastel « Le Café-Concert. Les Ambassadeurs » (1876-77) is among the master-pieces of the paintings dedicated to this theme. What Degas creates here has been reduced to a most brilliantly successful formula; this is the whole exciting, magical world of tinselly glamour of the metropolitan Café-Concert, a breath-taking moment in the life of a world of light, created by a thousand effects of light and

12) MAX LIEBERMANN, Gesammelte Schriften, Berlin 1922, p. 77.
13) JOHN REWALD, *Geschichte des Impressionismus,* Zurich-Stuttgart 1957, p. 187.

HORSE AND JOCKEY. Pencil.
Boymans Museum, Rotterdam.

At the Races. Pastel, 1883. (18" × 26"),
National Gallery of Art Ottawa, Canada

MARY CASSATT AT THE LOUVRE. Pastel on grey paper. (26" × 19"),
Coll. Henry McIlhenny, Museum of Art, Philadelphia ▷

DANCING GIRL LEAVING
HER DRESSING ROOM.
Pastel, about 1881.
($21^1/_4$" $\times$ $12^1/_2$"),
The Niarchos Collection

The Blue Dancers. Pastel, 1890. (33½" × 26"), The Louvre Museum, Paris

Two Dancers. Pastel on paper, about 1895. (45" × 41"),
Museum of Art, Dresden, Germany

Dancers at the Bar. Oil, 1888. (51" × 38"),
Duncan Phillips Memorial Gallery, Washington, D.C.

Group of Dancing Girls. Charcoal.

BALLET GIRLS IN SALMON-PINK SKIRTS. Pastel, about 1897. (35" ×25⅝")
▷ Coll. Mr. and Mrs. George Friedland, Merion, Pennsylvania

Study of a Nude. Charcoal.

brilliance. A similar theme, but without the same gay spirit, appears in the famous « Café-Boulevard Montmartre ». One looks out from inside on to the boulevard at night, out into a lonely, sad night in the town, as someone passes by, unreal, like a dark shadow. In front of the café sit the prostitutes, waiting for customers, full of the « resigned boredom and patience of the professional ». Degas offers a final solution for the interior: the setting is no longer a room that can offer protection and comfort; it is now open to the outside world, to the street, and therefore it follows that the people who are to be found there are homeless. It represents the life of slum-dwellers. This was followed by another painting of the same period, « L'Absinthe ». Apart from the social criticism and comment that this picture arouses, a feeling which may well bring to mind Zola's novel « L'Assomoir », which is a powerful and vivid protest against drink because of the tragedies that it causes. This is a picture that describes the human form itself with alarming strength and conviction. Two guests are left in the Café, seated in the upper right-hand corner of the picture, and although they are inside the room, they are symbols of grey superficiality, like the street mirrored in the background. A gaping void surrounds the couple — the actress Ellen Andrée and the etcher Marcellin Desboutin were the models although this is not really a portrait of them. Rather do they represent anonymous people, human symbols of a nameless destiny. Gotthard Jedlicka has been able to describe the abyss of hopelessness in « L'Absinthe » in a most vivid way: « the emptiness of the void is made visible in the painting ». In no other known work of European Painting does this feeling appear with such intensity. The spiritual atmosphere which has been created here is the very opposite of the mixture of well-being and self-confidence that can be seen in the paintings of the Impressionists. Yet this painting dates from the early period of Impressionism. The mood which Degas wanted to capture was the flight of two people into a companionship in which their loneliness becomes so tangible that it shocks one [14]. The painting with the misleading title « Le Voie », which refers perhaps to a scene in Zola's novel « Madeleine Féral » can be placed in mood very near to that of « L'Absinthe »; Madeleine says to Francis: « You suffer, because you love me — and I cannot be yours ». This was a great prophecy of one of the basic themes of « fin de siecle » painting, which Lautrec and Munch, particulary, were later to formulate.

« Le Café Boulevard Montmartre », « L'Absinthe », « Le Voie », as well as several paintings set in the brothel, are linked by the fact that they describe low slum life and relate this to another cycle of subjects, which is one of the fundamental characteristics of Degas. He describes the low-class working person, this time with a direct and unadorned approach to life rather than in « bohemian » style, which always bears a trace of the Romantic. His series of paintings dealing with ironing-women, milliners, precedes Daumier's iconography ... The latter gives the worker a mythical, heroic appearance, moved by unsentimental love. Out of deep compassion, he recognizes his greatness even in his misery [15]. For Degas, however, this heroic aspect of every-day work no longer has a meaning. In the « Ironing Women » of 1882, we find women of frightening ugliness; in their dull, banal work, repose and physical exertion are contrasted in the two figures; one is leaning with all her force on the iron, while the other yawns and stretches herself; her wide-open mouth is a snapshot of truly disillusioning, fabulous vulgarity — these working women are portrayed as harridans. The desire for the ugly is toned down

14) Gotthard Jedlicka, *Degas « L'Absinthe »*, in: *Pariser Tagebuch*, Frankfurt on Main 1953.
15) Hans Seldmayr, *Grosse und Elend des Menschen*, Vienna 1948, p. 64.

in the paintings of the milliners, who are nevertheless caught in the most absurd positions, surrounded by coloured hats and often by slanting mirrors placed at the edge; these women are completely immersed in their activity of tryng on hats, so that any possibility of representative dignity is lost. Neither fashionable, social elegance of dress nor feminine charm must be depicted. These scenes already contain the idea which Degas, from 1880 on, working constantly and earnestly, later concentrates on for more than two decades: women at their toilette. The 19th-Century French painters did not favour feminine beauty to the extent of 18th-Century art. It is sufficient to remember the adoration with which Manet describes the Parisians — or the tenderness with which Renoir overwhelms the women in his painting. There is no trace of any of this left in Degas; nor is he influenced by the heathen cult of the female body or by the Chassériau's´ lust for the portrayal of the satisfied lover; with him we find intimacy without the intimate being shown, the animal without sensuality; with Degas the woman appears like an animal washing itself ([16]).

The paintings of women bathing, washing themselves, drying (and rubbing) themselves, combing their hair or being combed, are mainly seen from behind. They don't seem to heed their intimate positions in the boudoir or in the bathroom. Lastly, it is a penetration into the women's most private sphere of existence. They are defencelessly delivered up to the curiosity of the observer, set down with pitiless analysis and « a certain cruelty » (Vollard) so that one could say of these pictures that they were painted through a keyhole. The observer is able to see these women in positions that often have something of the ridiculous, distorted postures which would otherwise be seen only by a doctor examining his patient ([17]). His contemporaries therefore criticised this disillusioning view of women; Huysmans, for example, who accuses Degas of having cast the greatest insult in the face of the 19th Century by dethroning the idolized woman, who until then, had been safe-guarded, and debasing her by showing her in the bath-tub in humiliating postures. In fact, Degas, of course, had no intention of humiliating or exposing women. Among his toilette-paintings there are some works of most wonderfully-balanced and harmonious quality, such as « La Toilette » (Havemeyer Collection, Metropolitan Museum, New York), in which the woman happily offers her beaming body to the light. Again, it is the movement and its reproduction that interests him primarily. Something like a true « Encyclopedia » was the outcome of this: all the conceivable positions and expressions of a woman in the bathroom. Degas' world of themes — his iconography — whether the race course, the ballet, the theatre, the proletariat, or milliner-women at their toilette, derives its unity from the following fact: that it is always an anonymous person that appears, completely absorbed by an occupation which almost invariably coincides with a particular kind of movement. The human body is shown not so much for the body itself as for the movement. It does not appear endowed with individual personality, with a will of its own. Rather is it identified with one phase of existence; and that is why, necessarily, the general movement of the body has this anonymous quality.

The form peculiar to this art is made to serve this specific view of the human body. Degas, like almost all the impressionists, makes a point of showing the room in a naturalistic, illusionistic perspective, but he exaggerates and changes the scheme of the impressionistic view in the picture by means of slanting lines and sharp abridgements. It is an absolutely new feeling of space that Degas

16) PIERRE CABANNE, Munich, p. 213.
17) FRITZ LAUFER, *Das Interieur in der Malerei des 19. Jahrhunderts*, 1952, p. 213.

Study for the Painting "Coiffure". Charcoal.

depicts. He conceives the room as an inanimate thing, into which the figures have been placed and where they must hold their own vivid movement. With Lautrec and Munch, it is this feeling of space which is emphasized and which determines 20th-Century art. The necessary complement to this conception of the room is a phenomenon like overlapping, including, that is, in the picture, the fragmentary — an affinity with the photographer's « snapshot ». Fénéon has formulated all this as « *Cinématique infaillible* », and « *le Moderne exprimé* ». Apart from the emphasis on the room, these principles of composition always guarantee the maintenance of a balanced colour-scheme. Without doubt they were strongly inspired by the Japanese coloured wood-cut. Since Bracquemond, in 1856, had discovered the first wood-cuts of Hokusai, the artist's attention was drawn to this characteristic branch of Japanese art. Although the Japanese vogue reached its zenith later with Gauguin, van Gogh, Toulouse-Lautrec, Bonnard and Vuillard, Degas was the first to be impressed so profoundly by this newly-discovered form, whether it was the graphic style and subtlety of the lines, the generally decorative dress, off-centre distribution of the figures, or the « Fragment-principle » of the Japanese wood cut.

« Light » could be called the central theme of Impressionistic painting ([18]). It is used in representing landscape — as an element of revealing naturalism, which manifests itself as a superior encompassing factor. The light distracts the attention from the personal element, be it human being or thing, and emphasizes the pervading atmosphere of the picture. The impressionist system of brush-strokes, does not clearly outline the figure or design, but rather merges colours in an indistinct form, giving a vibrating effect. Far into the 70's Degas made use of shadow, giving it an earthen, clay colour, spotted with grey. Furthermore, he always emphasized the sketch as a necessary artistic means for the expression of movement, thus separating himself from the set principles of Impressionism. « The dancer is for me only an excuse to draw », and « Drawing is not form, but a way of seeing the form »; such remarks bear witness to almost a mania for drawing. The structure of his drawing has nothing of the indistinct, vibrating effect, characteristic of the Impressionists. About 1880, his silver-grey tones disappear more and more; they are replaced by brilliant red and reddish-yellow tones of light; the dull colours give place to warm ones, and pastel becomes the principle medium in this change of style. Degas' turn towards the pastel took place by degrees; till 1869, it had only been a technical means for him; but about 1875-76, he uses pastel for important pictures, and after 1880-85 it predominates. Oil colour no longer seems to interest him very much — or else it is used to simulate the effects of the pastel with its softening, hazy quality, as for instance in the « Portrait of Woman with Red Shawl » (1886). Manet and Renoir also used pastel, but only from time to time — at random. Degas is the only painter who makes it his primary means of expression. He wins a position for pastel which calls to mind the great pastel period of the 18th Century. Degas recognized in pastel a medium which struck the balance between drawing and painting, which enables him to draw while painting — and paint while drawing. Degas made the utmost of the possibilities offered by pastel; furthermore, he combined it with other techniques: with gouache, water-colour and « peinture à l'essence » (terpentine-painting), and even with monotype. Through the use of pastel, Degas finally achieved a certain blending of colours on the surface. He applied thin layers of different colours of paint and pastel, each layer of which is separately sprayed with fixative, and a relief of heavy thick paste. At first, this technique shows a relationship to the comma-like structure of colour used by the Impressionists, but in the later pastels he turns away

18) Fritz Novothny, *Die grossen französischen Impressionisten*, Vienna, 1952, p. 13.

82

Dancing Girl. Study. Pastel.

from completely naturalistic and illusionistic concept, and his paintings assume the characteristic of a shower-like spray and are imbued with fiery pastel-tones in swirls of colour. The dark tones no longer exist; the colour gives a shimmering effect, like a dance of patches and spots, and forms the line of the drawing, which is now shown in streams of colour-lines that reduce body and room to their elementary, basic form. This does not mean, however, that the movement of the ballerinas and the women at their toilette, are not depicted as accurately as they were before. However, both the sharply-observed progress of movement and the bengalic illumination and exotic quality of colour give the later works an unreal effect, and the figures appear somewhat ghost-like and diabolic — in this he far outstripped all other impressionistic endeavours. Herein lies the modern quality in Degas' later works, bringing them close to Fauvism as a fundamental trend in 20th-Century art.

There is nothing much to say about the master's personal life. After his return from America, he sought out a group of Impressionists, and joined their first Exhibition in 1874, and the following one as well, although his remarks became increasingly critical regarding his relationship to the programmatical Impressionists: « I have always tried to bring my colleagues to see the possibilities offered by drawing — which I esteem more effective than colour — but they wouldn't listen » [19]. In 1874, his father died, leaving the bank in a rather difficult financial situation, and in the following years his brothers suffered additional heavy losses through bad business management. This made Degas decide to sell part of his collection in order to help them — a fact which distressed him very much and which he regarded as a blight on the family honour. The gap which this left in his collection he soon filled, however, for he was, all through his life, an avid collector of infallible judgement and taste. For a time he thought of bequeathing his entire collection, but because of the depressing effect the Gustave Moreau Museum had on him, he decided to dismiss the idea. After his death, the collection was auctioned; among the paintings he owned were two Grecos, one Cuyp, and above all, pictures by Ingres, Delacroix, Corot, Cézanne, Manet, Mary Cassatt, Pissarro, Sisley, Renoir, Gauguin, van Gogh; quite apart from the numerous works of his closest friends Bartholomé and the Rouarts.

After 1885, Degas was disturbed by the increasing loss of his eyesight. Nevertheless, he continued to travel a great deal. In 1887, for instance, he went with Boldini to Spain and Morocco, and, in 1890, with Bartholomé he toured Burgundy. But, after 1892, his illness entered a critical phase, and he was already forced to give up oil-painting. In about 1904-06, Degas was almost completely blind. It was at this time that these bitter words were spoken: « Everything is trying for a blind man who wants to make believe that he can see... » It was almost impossible for him to paint, and, although his hand and spirit were still alive and agile, his dimming vision prevented any further work. Degas had to confine himself to retouching former paintings. Yet, even now, he created new works of great value and broad design, which is shown in his later works, and which is (because of his illness) a last attempt at expressing himself artistically. He finds most consolation in the sculpturing of statuettes — ballerinas and horses. With these sculptures, which cannot be honoured here, Degas makes advances into the future of sculptural design; through them he joins the ranks of the great painter-sculptors of the 19th Century, who are the most important forerunners of the *avant-garde* sculpture of the 20th Century. The loneliness in which Degas had always been immersed became overwhelming in his last years. One

19) Burlington Magazine, Nov. 1917.

Dancing Girl. Study. Charcoal.

Study of a Nude. Charcoal.

Study of a Woman Combing. Charcoal.

after another, his friends died and finally, in 1912, his most intimate friend, Henri Rouart, too, passed away. The same year, Degas was forced to give up his studio in the rue Victor-Massé. It was Suzanne Valadon who got a new apartment for him in the boulevard de Clichy. He could still enjoy the fact that, with the Camondo Collection, in 1914, a great many of his most remarkable works were recognized.

In his last years he could no longer work. For hours he would wander alone through the town he loved so much. Photographs, which Bartholomé, the last of his living friends, took of him in 1915, show Degas as a kind of blind Homer, full of a spiritual moving force in his expression, which explains why Arsène Alexandre den Verleigh was able to compare him to King Lear. The man, who left this earth on the 27th of September 1917, had outlived his purpose. The world took little notice of his death, immersed as it was in the great happenings of the war. In itself, his personal life was of little importance; it served merely as an instrument for the expression of his creative art.

RUSSIAN DANCING-GIRLS. Pastel, c. 1897 (32" × 21"), Former Coll. Ambroise Vollard, Paris

BIBLIOGRAPHY

Caricature. Collection Daniel Halevy. Editions des Quatre Chemins, Paris.

C. MAUCLAIR, *Edgar Degas*, in « Revue de l'Art Ancien et Moderne », November 1903.

P. A. LEMOISNE, *Degas*, Paris 1912.

W. SICKERT, *Degas*, in: « Burlington Magazine », 1917, pp. 183-191.

A. ALEXANDRE, *Essai sur Monsieur Degas*, in: « Les Arts », No. 166, pp. 2-24.

P. JAMOT, *Degas*, Paris, in: « Gazette des Beaux-Arts », June 1918.

P. LAFOND, *Degas*, Paris 1919.

H. HERTZ, *Degas*, Paris 1920.

J. MEIER-GRAEFE, *Degas*, Munich 1920.

P. A. LEMOISNE, *Les Carnets de Degas au Cabinet des Estampes*, in: « Gazette des Beaux-Arts », April 1921.

H. RIVIÈRE, *Les dessins de Degas*, Paris 1922-23.

G. COQUIOT, *Degas*, Paris 1924.

P. JAMOT, *Degas* 1924.

A. VOLLARD, *Degas*, Paris 1924.

J. B. MANSON, *The Life and Work of Edgar Degas*, London 1927.

L'Amour de l'Art, special number on Degas, July 1931.

M. GUÉRIN, *Lettres de Degas, recueillies et annotées*, Paris 1931.

G. JEANNIOT, *Souvenirs sur Degas*, in: « Revue Universelle », Oct.-Nov. 1933.

J. WALKER, *Degas et les Maîtres anciens*, in: Gazette des Beaux-Arts », 1933, II. p. 173-185.

A. ANDRÉ, *Degas*, Paris 1935.

Caricature. Collection Daniel Halevy. Editions des Quatre Chemins, Paris.

G. Rivière, *M. Degas de Paris*, Paris 1935.

G. Grappe, *Degas*, Paris 1936.

P. Valéry, *Degas*, Paris 1937.

C. Mauclair, *Degas*, Paris 1937.

E. Rouart, *Degas*, in: « Le Point », Feb. 1937.

Catalogue of the Degas Exhibition, Paris, Musée de l'Orangerie, March-April 1937.

J. Rewald, *Degas*, Paris 1937.

W. Vanbeselaere, *Degas*, Brussels 1941.

W. Rotzle, *Zehn Ballettstudien von Edgar Degas*, Bâle 1948.

W. Hausenstein, *Degas*, Berne 1948.

M. Rebatet, *Degas*, Paris 1944.

J. Rewald, *Degas and his family in New Orleans*, in: « Gazette des Beaux-Arts », August 1946.

H. Graber, *Degas nach eigenen und fremden Zeugnissen*, Bâle 1942.

D. Rouart, *Degas à la recherche de sa technique*, Paris 1945.

J. Rewald, *The realism of Degas*, in: « Magazine of Art », Jan. 1946.

J. Lassaigne, *Edgar Degas*, Paris 1947.

J. Leymarie, *Les Degas au Louvre*, Paris 1947.

J. Leymarie, *Les dessins de Degas*, Paris 1948.

P. A. Lemoisne, *Degas et son oeuvre*, Paris 1946-49.

D. Rouart, *Degas*, Paris 1949.

J. Fèvre, *Mon oncle Degas*. Memoirs and documents edited by P. Borel, Geneva 1949.

L. Browse, *Degas Dancers*, London 1949.

H. Dumont, *Degas*, New York-Paris 1950.

L. Fergusson, *Degas Dancers*, London 1950.

D. Cooper, *Pastels by Edgar Degas*, Bâle 1952.

B. Champigneulle, *Dessins de Degas*, Paris 1952.

R. Huyghe-L. Huyghe, *Degas*, Paris 1953.

R. Rey, *Degas*, Paris 1954.

F. Fosca, *Degas*, Geneva 1954.

P. A. Lemoisne, *Degas et son oeuvre*, Paris 1954.

P. A. Lemoisne, *Degas, peintre des chevaux*, in: « Le Jardin des Arts », July 1955.

C. Roger-Marx, *Degas, Danseuses*, Paris 1956.

J. Rewald, *Degas, Das Plastische Werk*, Zurich 1957.

J. Sutherland Boggs, *Degas' Notebooks at the Bibliothèque Nationale*, I: Groupe A (1853-58); II: Group B (1858-61), in « Burlington Magazine » 1958, pp. 163-171, 196-205.

P. Cabanne, *Edgar Degas*, Paris 1958.

M. Sérullaz, *Degas, femmes a leur toilette*, Paris 1958.

D. C. Rich, *Edgar Degas*, Cologne 1959.

ILLUSTRATIONS